WITH JESUS
I Share

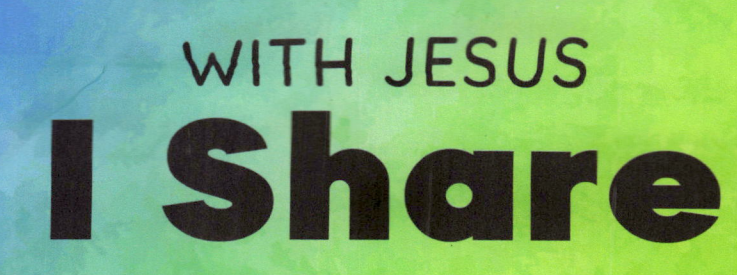

Copyrights

Copyright 2022 by Good News Meditations Kids - All rights reserved

This book or parts thereof may not be reproduced in any form, stored in any retrieval system, or transmitted in any form by any means—electronic, mechanical, photocopy, recording, or otherwise—without prior written permission of the copyright holder.

www.gnmkids.com

This book belongs to:

....

....

When Carlos and Daddy got to the park, Carlos ran to the sandbox and started playing with his toy car. Maria, his neighbor, ran up to Carlos.

"That's a cool toy! Can I play?" She asked.

"No, you can't play with me! If I give you a turn, I'll never see how fast it can go," Carlos yelled.

"Did you know that a little boy gladly helped Jesus feed 5,000 people?" asked daddy

"One day while Jesus was teaching, everyone became hungry. Jesus saw a little boy who had five loaves of bread and two fish. The boy shared his lunch to help Jesus feed everyone. Jesus multiplied the food so that there was enough for everyone." Daddy explained.

The next day, Maria arrived at the park and asked Carlos if she could to play with his toy. Carlos remembered the story of Jesus and the little boy, and shares his toy with Maria. Her face lit up instantly with excitement. Before long, they were all having fun!

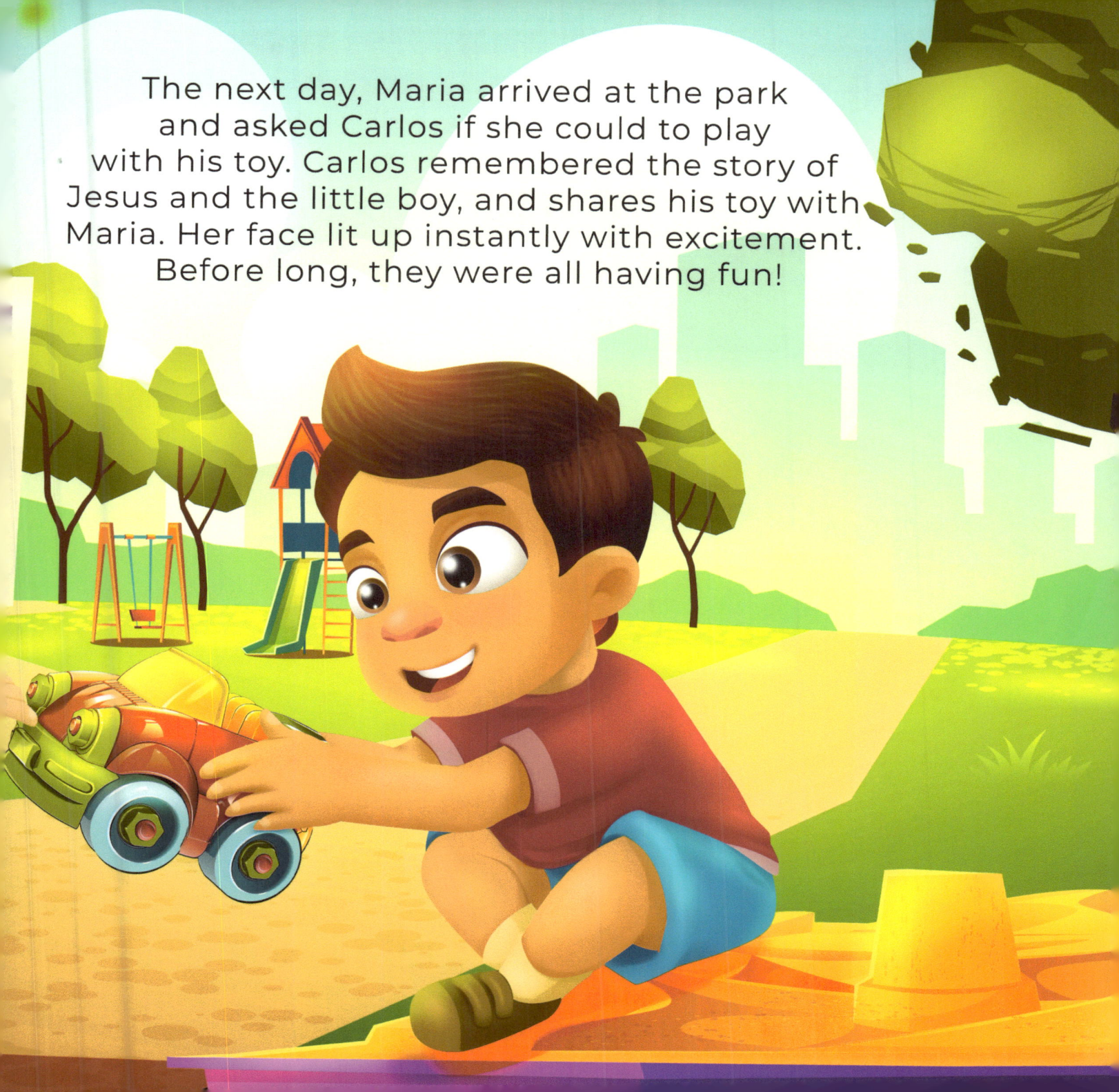

Daddy noticed and asked his son why he shared his toy.

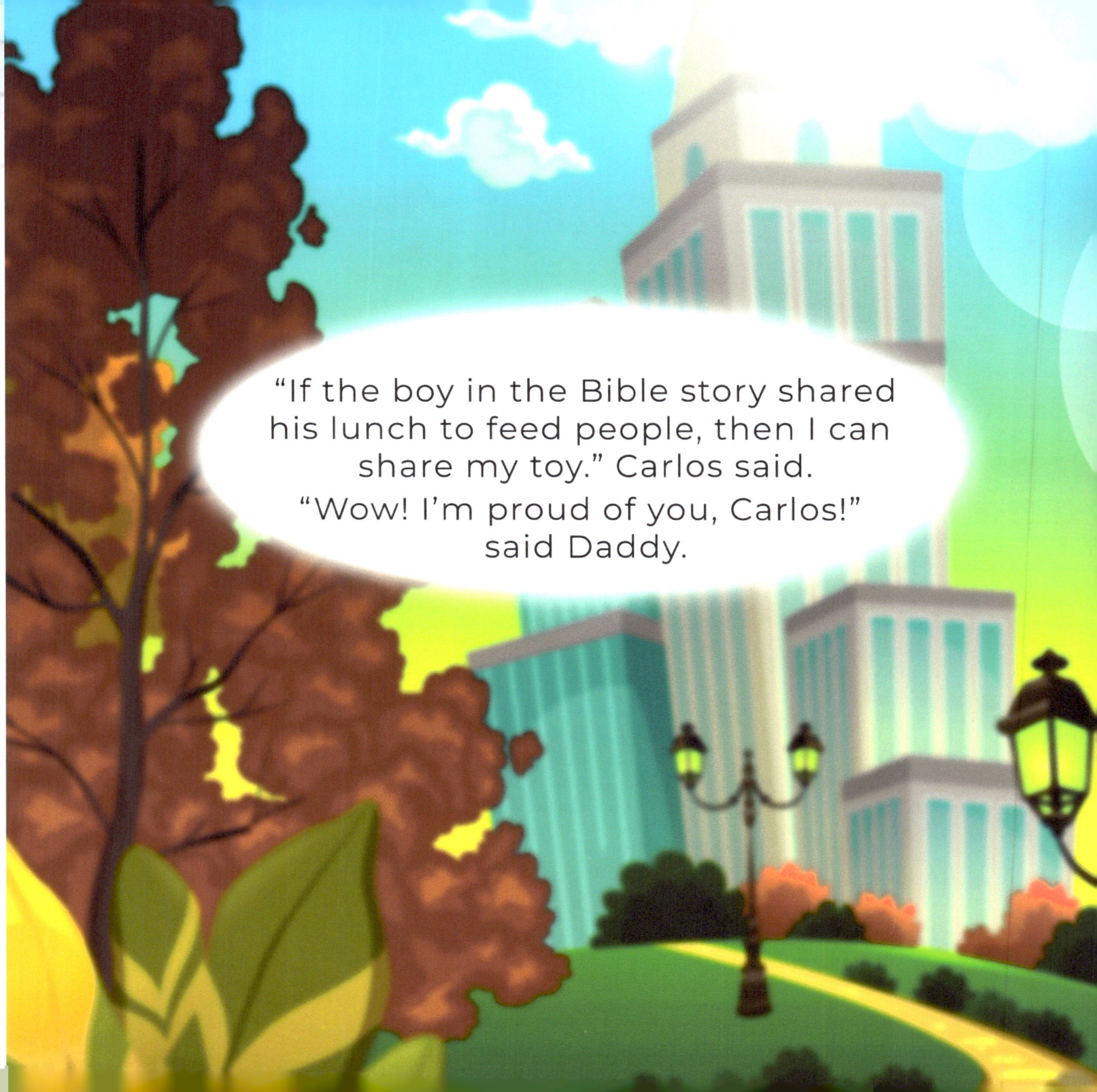

"If the boy in the Bible story shared his lunch to feed people, then I can share my toy." Carlos said.

"Wow! I'm proud of you, Carlos!" said Daddy.

"It felt good to share my new toy. Maria even taught me how to make it go faster," said Carlos.

As Carlos about to go to bed that night, Daddy gave him a big hug and told him, "Sharing with others always brings joy."
The End.

"And do not forget to do good and to share with others, for with such sacrifices God is pleased"

Hebrews 13v16 (KJV)

Author's note:

Thank you so much for reading this book. If you enjoyed this book, we would love it if you could leave a review or recommend it to a friend.

If you want the coloring book or the audiobook for free please visit:
www.gnmkids.com

Thank you for your support!
Please checkout our other books

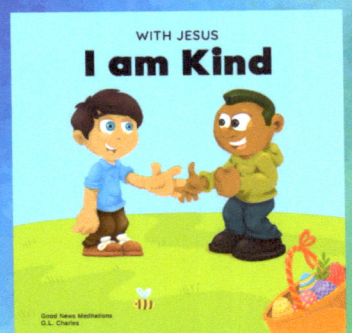

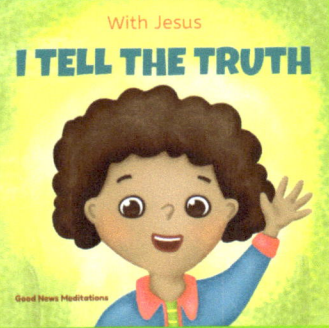

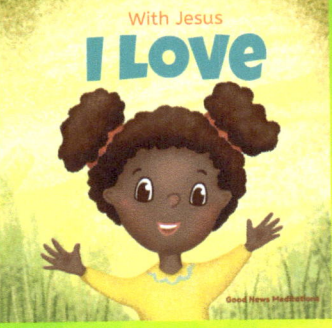
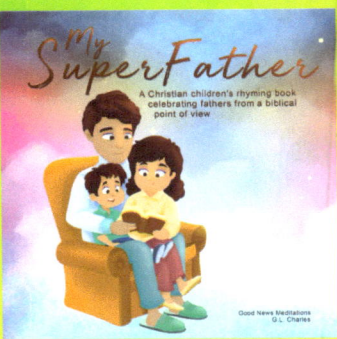

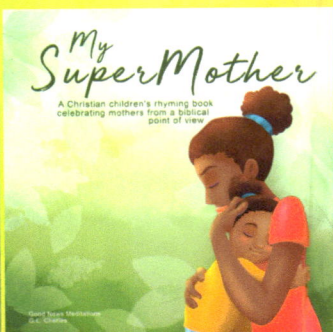

www.gnmkids.com